Dear Elaine

The

unvarnished

truth about

me!

Enjoy

Beyond the CHOKECHERRY TREE

A JOURNEY FROM THE TOP OF A SMALL TREE TO THE REST OF THE UNIVERSE

a memoir

JOHN M. DELEHANTY

BEYOND THE CHOKECHERRY TREE

A JOURNEY FROM THE TOP OF A SMALL TREE TO THE REST OF THE UNIVERSE

ISBN: 979-8-35090-638-7

This book is dedicated to Judy,

the love of my life

Contents

Introduction

BEYOND THE CHOKECHERRY TREE

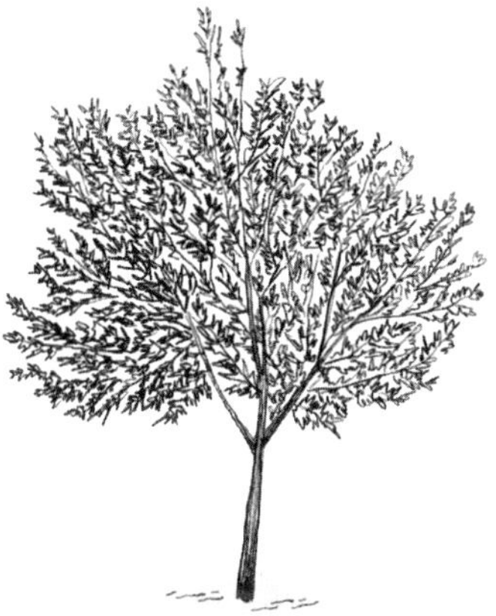

When I was eight, I could see my whole world from the top of the chokecherry tree in my neighbor's backyard. Although it only stretched for a few blocks from Blessed Sacrament Church to Helen Street School and the Hamden Library, it was a safe happy place which I never wanted to leave.

When I was 12, my family moved to another state and I had to leave the chokecherry tree behind. Even without the tree, my new world was much the same. It was cabined by Saint Francis Xavier Church, South Junior High and the Fogg Library.

I was a very white, very Catholic, very immature young man. But I had an intuitive knack for correctly answering multiple choice questions. That talent, my only one, got me into Brown University, a much larger world than the one I left.

I stumbled at first but ultimately coped. I met my first Jewish person (my roommate) and my first Black person, and went on my first date. I drank my first beer, my first whiskey, and my first vodka, all at once. I learned much about the world I never knew, and, driven by an urge to escape my past, worked very hard to succeed in my studies.

Brown opened the door to law school, where my transformation shifted into a higher gear. I was still hauling around my past—Catholicism, whiteness and small-town myopia. But then I met Judy.

She was beautiful, refined and Jewish, and carried none of the baggage that I was burdened with. And, most important of all, she wanted to marry me. She enlarged my world far beyond anything I had known.

But marrying Judy and leaving my past behind exacted a very high price. I became estranged from my parents and younger brother, abandoned the Irishness that was written all over my freckled face, and struggled to shoehorn my name, Delehanty, into my new Jewish world. Decades later, although I have transformed, the two external worlds I still inhabit—the old and the new—are still trying to figure out who I am.

I have written this collection of stories to illustrate how I evolved from the little boy atop the chokecherry tree to the person I am today. I hope you enjoy them.

Chapter 1

DELIA

I have always been comfortable in the company of women, particularly older ones. This may be because two of the people who gave me unconditional love early in life were my grandmothers, Delia and Adelaide. This story is about Delia.

Delia grew up in a white-washed, thatch-roofed cottage in Miltown Malbay, County Clare, Ireland, a place of dazzling green beauty on the cliffs overlooking the Atlantic. Delia's home was a stone's throw from the boiling ocean, where the Spanish Armada had foundered on the rocks and most of its sailors drowned. She emigrated from her hard-scrabble one-cow farm and crossed that ocean to New Haven Connecticut, where she was a housemaid in the mansion of a Yale professor. She barely finished the sixth grade, but she brought with her a broad smile, a lilting brogue, bright blue eyes and clear pale skin the color of parchment. She also brought her Catholic faith which encased her like a straitjacket, the laces of which were her daily recitation of the Rosary.

She met my grandfather, John Delehanty, at a County Clare Dance in New Haven. The Irish character is like two-sided coin: Delia was the gregarious side with her infectious laugh; John was the reverse, a gruff resentful man, forever cursing the British and their subjugation of the Irish race. But John was a good provider. He got a job as a trolley driver and Delia quit her job with the Professor. She soon had her own two-family house, with tenants, no less. She started having babies right away, first James and then my father, another John. Although she had left the raging Atlantic, Delia could not escape the quieter but just as deadly Quinnipiac River. Little James, age five, wandered down Grand Avenue, fell in and drowned. John was two. Anne came after, but Delia was never the same. The beads on her Rosary were worn down with her constant fingering.

My father grew up; endured parochial school, a distant father and a fearful mother; went to college; was bailed out by FDR and the Civilian Conservation Corps (an antidote to the Depression); married my Methodist mother; and in 1942 was called to war. John senior died two months later and my mother, alone, gave Delia the moral support she could not find in the Church.

I was Delia's first grandchild. I had her blue eyes and pale freckled skin; and my ears stuck out just like hers. We spent summers together at Aunt Anne's house in the country. I slept in Delia's attic room with my father's graduation tassel hanging from a lamp over my head. We said the Rosary together. I was almost as fanatical about Catholicism as she was. She paid her room and board by cleaning Anne's house and taking care of the cats. I was her helper, but my privileges had their limits. The cats got real milk; I got the powdered kind. Anne and Bill lived a cut above my family. They had a cocktail every night and let me watch. Delia was never invited. She was in her room with her prayer book.

I really didn't care for the cocktail hour. I preferred playing canasta with Delia, hearing her brogue, listening to her laugh and just being in her warm, enveloping presence. At that point in her life she had become quite large and bosomy, filling out her housedress, the only piece of clothing she wore except on Sundays. My favorite part of the week was our walk around the corner to the country store for a vanilla ice cream cone, which always seemed like a miracle to me, followed by a visit to her friend from Ireland for tea. The two of them would reminisce about the old country while I read some *National Geographic* magazines. Delia loved to show me off and brag to her friend about how well I was doing in school. After tea, the two of them would read the tea leaves. They loved to joke about the girl I would marry, whose face they could see in the soppy brown leaves. I could never make out the face and, at age 10, I didn't really care.

James's death under water followed Delia and her offspring like a ghost. She never set foot in water, nor did my father unless he had to. I did not learn to swim until I was 12, subconsciously haunted by fear of drowning until someone threw me in over my head. Her caution extended to anything my brothers or I wanted to do that involved even a smidgen of risk, like riding a bike.

The last time I saw Delia she was dead. She was subjected to the gruesome custom of an open casket, surrounded by expensive bouquets and a kneeler, where the mourners said goodbye and kissed her cold, alabaster face. I will never forget getting the call about her death. I was on a pond playing hockey with college friends when someone came by and said there was a call for me, a rare occasion at that time. I was devastated. This was the first death of a person close to me. Even more difficult for me was the wake, where friends and relatives drank and ate within a few feet of Delia's body. I felt very lonely in that crowd, wanting them all to go away so that I could spend a few moments alone with Delia.

Those moments never came. I have since moved very far away from some of the things that Delia held dear, like the Catholic Church. But much of her is in me, which I am reminded of every time I look in a mirror.

Chapter 2

ADELAIDE

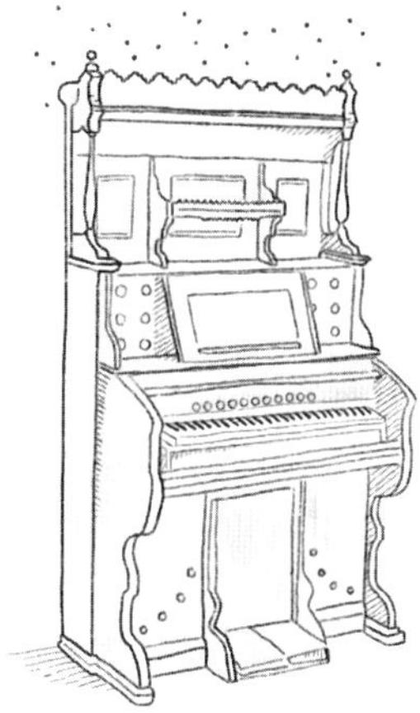

I never knew either of my grandfathers. They both died well before I was born. But I was blessed with two grandmothers who both lived well into my adulthood and enriched it immensely. They could not have been more different.

Delia, my father's mother, was short, plump, pale and freckled, with a lovely soft brogue and an infectious smile. Adelaide, my maternal grandmother, was tall, had dark skin, a very prominent nose, long arms and long thin fingers. Her thin wavy hair sat like a bird's nest on the top of her head. She looked like she could have been an Iroquois squaw, but she would not have liked that comparison. Unlike Delia, she wore her Methodist religion lightly. For Adelaide, the main function of the Church next door was to house the organ which her slim dancing fingers played with gusto, as she did the piano, all self-taught.

Her birth name was Nelson. The family story is that her father was a Norwegian sailor who disembarked in New Haven and married a local Yankee girl. Forget the Iroquois, Adelaide was a Viking! She married Hugh McDonald, another Yankee who had emigrated from Maine in the early 1900s. Hugh was a small-time entrepreneur, tobacconist, pharmacist—whatever brought in a few bucks. He and Adelaide must have enjoyed each other. He took her out in his big car, bought her that house on East Pearl Street next to the Church, and the two of them produced six children in the next 15 years, including my mother, who Adelaide called Virginia because she was as dark as Adelaide was.

Unfortunately, Hugh brought with him from Maine a genetic kidney disease which had killed most of the McDonalds before they were 50. Hugh was no exception. He died suddenly of an aneurysm, a side effect of the disease, at age 45, leaving Adelaide with nothing other than the house on East Pearl Street and six kids, ranging in age from 16 to one. Donald, the eldest son, went to work to support the family. Although he was at the top of his class in high school, college was out of the question.

Adelaide went to work too, sewing ties in a factory in New Haven. Her eldest daughter Phyllis soon joined her there. The two of them were inseparable for the rest of their lives. Donald eventually bought Adelaide a cozy four-room cottage on the outskirts of New Haven, where she and Phyllis lived together for 30 years. Another son, Scotty, bought the house next to the Church.

Hugh's early death was hardly ever mentioned, but it was clear that all six McDonald children (and eventually their 12 children) worshipped Adelaide, and rightly so. She was someone you wanted to be near. Why? She never judged, never criticized and at least for the grandchildren she was a strong and indulgent buffer against our own overbearing parents.

Case in point. When I was eight, I decided that I wanted to take a trip on my new bike. A friend and I biked 10 miles to Adelaide's house without mentioning it to our parents. Adelaide's response could not have been better. She did not say a word about the risks or dangers of this excursion, which actually was quite foolish for an eight-year-old; she just offered us some blueberry pie right from the oven. Eventually our parents found us, but Adelaide would never rat us out.

I must have remembered that trip when I was in college. I was at school in Providence and my date went to college in New London, a one-hour train ride away. Her curfew was at midnight. Caught up in our mooning over each other, we miscalculated the arrival time in New London. What to do? Go to Adelaide's house! We stayed on the train until we got to New Haven at 2 a.m. Adelaide was nonplussed when we arrived at her door. My date slept in Phyllis's bed, Phyllis slept with Adelaide, and I slept up in the attic. Adelaide made us pancakes for breakfast and never said a word about this visit to you know who.

That Adelaide's house was a haven was fostered every Christmas when all 26 McDonalds, spouses and kids packed into the tiny green cottage to exchange gifts and sing as Adelaide played piano. Everyone lived nearby except my family, but we made the journey from Massachusetts every year. My two brothers and I loved dozing on Adelaide's floor in our sleeping bags. Although our parents were in the next room, we were in Adelaide's house and that made all the difference.

Adelaide lived a very long life. Ninety-six years was a remarkable span three decades ago. Her infectious love of life and unflappable calm carried her a very long way. But even the most optimistic mother finds it hard to witness the death of her children, even if they are well into adulthood. Adelaide buried three of her children, all victims of Hugh's disease, before she herself let go. I cherish the sanctuary and unqualified love that she brought to me every time I was with her.

Chapter 3

THE HUMMEL AND THE HAT

Sitting on a shelf directly above the desk on which I write are a three-inch tall Hummel figure of a young boy singing and a US Army cavalry hat. The boy has blond hair and blue eyes and is nattily dressed in a green jacket and red bow tie. In his right hand he holds the page of notes from which he is singing; his left hand is casually stuck in his pants pocket. He looks to be about seven years old. The hat is dark khaki color with a wide brim and a crown with three indentations. It looks like the hat Teddy Roosevelt wore when he stormed San Juan Hill.

The Hummel belonged to my mother Virginia; the hat was my father John's. These two treasures bring back to life memories of each of them and their lives together.

They married a month before Dad went off to the war in Europe. He had been in ROTC in college so he was Second Lieutenant when he left in 1942. The army was a reprieve. Dad had barely been employed in the five years since he graduated from UConn. One year, thanks to FDR, he planted firs and spruce in Wyoming as part of the Civilian Conservation Corps; that was pretty much it.

Although he was an officer in the cavalry, Dad had no interest in shooting anyone. But the men in his platoon did. They were all from Kentucky. Dad's unit, Ordnance, protected and supplied the heavy weapons to the front lines. They were a rich target for the Germans. The Kentucky sharpshooters did their best to keep the Krauts, as Dad called them, at bay. Dad and his men fought their way through Algeria, Tunisia, Sicily and Italy, all the way to Rome. They took Rome on the day before D-Day. Dad and his platoon got one day of glory when they marched into the Eternal City in June 1944. The next day, to Dad's chagrin, they were upstaged by the much bigger story at the English Channel.

Dad formed strong opinions during the war. He distrusted the Arabs in Algeria and Tunisia whom he viewed as thieves and cowards. He loved the Italian soldiers who surrendered in droves rather than putting up a fight. And, even though they were shooting at him and his men, he admired the German soldiers who fought to the death. In his opinion, one German soldier was worth 100 Italians.

Mom wrote to him every day. She numbered each letter. There are 853 of them, all of which my brothers and I still have. Dad wrote back often as well, but he could not match Mom's blistering pace. My brother Dennis has scanned and archived every letter. I have read many of Mom's, but doing so made me feel like a voyeur, so I stopped. My parents were young and in love before being torn apart by the war. Mom's early letters are filled with sexual longing and intimacy, traits I rarely saw in her when I was growing up. She also had to deal with the death of Dad's father two months after he left for Europe; there were no hardship leaves in World War II.

While Dad was away, Mom finished her Master's Degree and began to teach second grade. Her students were all about the same age as the little boy captured in the Hummel figurine. Mom loved to sing, but she could not carry a tune. Her mother was a talented church organist and piano player. On Sundays, Mom joined the congregation in their full-throated Methodist hymns which drowned out her own offkey singing. The little Hummel boy looks like he is singing one of those hymns, which may explain why he was my mother's favorite.

After the victory in Rome, Dad came back to the States in the summer of 1944. He was stationed with Mom at a fort in Terre Haute, Indiana. He told me they were "fattening him up" for the invasion of Japan. John and Virginia made up for the two years of lost intimacy. I came into the world twelve months later. After Truman dropped the A-bombs, the Japanese invasion was called off. My parents took me back home to New Haven. I was only a Hoosier for twelve weeks.

The war was over, but the kinship it formed among the veterans and their wives blossomed. Dad came home a major in the army and enlisted in the army reserves for all of my childhood. My brothers and I took turns wearing the cavalry hat while Dad talked about the war. His stories were more wistful than vainglorious. His hair turned white at age 31 and he drank quarts of beer and whiskey shots like they were water. He got a job as a railway mail clerk, sorting bags of mail on the trains between Boston and New York. He was required to carry a handgun, but was afraid of it and what it could do if I or one of my brothers found it. He hid it away in the attic. Every summer he would go to Army camp in upstate New York and bring us back patches, hats and other khaki stuff. To us, the Army was really cool.

Mom was even more gung ho after the war than Dad was. She joined the auxiliaries of the VFW and the Amvets and marched in every Memorial Day parade. She loved to strut to John Sousa rhythms and sing along with the crowd. She imbued patriotism into her second graders all year, especially on Flag Day, her favorite holiday. One of the joys of teaching for Mom was that each year there was a new crop of seven-year-olds who looked like her never changing little Hummel. Although in each of the annual second grade class photos Mrs. Delehanty got a little older and grayer, everyone around her looked fresh, sparkling and bright.

My life with my parents became more complicated as I grew older. Dad was not happy when I quit the ROTC in college and turned my back on the military. Mom couldn't understand why she had to share my affections with my wife, Judy. But these are mere pebbles in the stream of time, and their once sharp edges worn smooth.

I still have the Hummel and the hat. They both serve as daily reminders of the strengths and sacrifices of my parents, without whom there would be no one to write this memoir.

Chapter 4

VIRGINIA, MY REFUGE

Virginia was Adelaide's fifth child, born into a family which could barely afford two. Her father Hugh was a jack of all trades from Maine, but he could never find steady work in New Haven. Hugh was a Scot, with sandy hair, a large nose with a bump right in the middle, and paper white skin. All of Adelaide's first four children looked like him. But Virginia had Adelaide's olive skin and thick dark hair. Adelaide thought she looked like a "darky" so she called her Virginia.

Hugh died of a stroke in 1925, when Virginia was seven and little sister Lynette was two. They say the twenties were roaring, but not for Adelaide. Hugh left her with six mouths to feed and little else. Fourteen-year-old Donald quit high school to support the family. Adelaide began sewing ties in the factory as soon as she could, and sister Phyllis, who never left Adelaide's side for the next 70 years, soon joined her.

The family's hardships hardly made a trace on Virginia's impish smiling face in all the photos taken of her in those difficult days. And there were many: Virginia at the beach, Virginia on a pony, Virginia picking flowers in the woods, Virginia dressed up for Church next door. Without a dime, she was buoyed up by Adelaide, her four older siblings, and the tight-knit flock of Methodists to which they all belonged. Throughout her life, Virginia always sang a tune, usually off-key. She was an embodiment of "Whistle a Happy Tune" long before Rodgers and Hammerstein gave that song to Anna and the King of Siam.

Virginia was as bright and ambitious as she was happy. No tie factory for her. Somehow, she got a BA from New Haven State Teachers College, the first and only person in her family to go to college, and then a Master's Degree at Yale, a very long way from her side of the tracks. She then married John, a Catholic guy who had also gone to college, and the two of them, led by Virginia, started the long slow climb up the ladder of social mobility. I was the first of her three sons. Virginia took a break from teaching to raise us and poured her heart and soul into me, Hugh, and Dennis.

John came back from the war seriously flawed, a struggling provider, an out of control drinker and a man who could not harness his fierce Irish temper. I will never forget the night he let me carry his bottle of whiskey home from the liquor store. I dropped it, spilling the precious liquid onto the sidewalk. His rage was frightening, fueled by all three of his demons: the cost of the bottle, the loss of the whiskey, and the knowledge that any solace it would bring that night was gone.

Virginia was my refuge and I hers. We talked for hours while she wallpapered and painted the house and taught me those skills. I helped her correct her second graders' papers and watched her skillfully draw horses, rabbits and other animals and print the next day's lesson which she would mimeograph at school. After classes in junior high school, rather than joining my friends, I would often go to Virginia's classroom and tell her about my day. I was enormously proud that "Mrs. Delehanty" was my mother and that she was looked upon with awe by her little charges while they were in her classroom and well after they had gone on to the next grades. Her imprint on me was enormous: education was to be taken seriously, it was the key to a happy and successful life, and I could never let her down.

Virginia loved a parade. She would happily march down Main Street with every single group, raising her chubby knees high in the air: the teachers, the Democrats, the Cub Scouts, the Veterans of Foreign Wars and the other Justices of the Peace. If the Catholics marched, she would have joined them too. And she loved flags, particularly the red, white and blue. Her favorite holiday was Flag Day on June 14. She would parade her flock of seven-year-olds around the school flagpole, have them recite the Pledge of Allegiance in their squeaky voices, and then lead them in a rousing chorus or two of "God Bless America," her favorite tune. Everyone else in the school joined in.

I often wonder why Virginia clung so tightly to all of these institutions. I think she saw them as providing security in the uncertain world into which she was born. School was a pathway out of poverty, the Democrats of FDR made sure that no one who lost a parent would be put out on the street, the Boy Scouts and the Church reinforced the moral values that she instilled at home. Most of all, America and its flag protected Virginia, her family and all those she loved from the dangerous world outside our borders.

I almost never cry. But I bawled for hours on a cold night in January 1978 when I learned that Virginia had glioblastoma, an incurable and inoperable brain tumor. During the next 14 months, all the parts of her body began to shut down, but the Virginia I knew and loved was gone as soon as I got that call. We buried her more than 40 years ago. But every single action she took while she was alive is part of me today. I still love a parade, proudly fly the flag, and, if pressed, can draw a very respectable looking horse. And, most of all, if my moral compass starts to get a little wobbly, I know where to turn.

After Virginia died, we set up a college scholarship for young women who planned to become elementary school teachers. My brothers and I are very happy to know that there are 40 little Virginias out there trying to do what she did so well.

Chapter 5

DESCENDING FROM ROYALTY

"We are descended from Kings," I would often hear my father's voice proclaim. When I was young, the irony of it went right over my head. My Irish grandfather was a dirt-poor farmer from County Clare who emigrated to New Haven Connecticut and ultimately became a trolley driver. My Irish grandmother was a maid to the WASP faculty members at Yale until she was able to buy her own modest home. They would have been much more comfortable in the servants' hall than in the drawing room with the royals. But the glorious, if imaginary, past was palpable—even if just as an antidote to the harshness of real life.

My father was a little more fortunate, but the "Kings" myth still persisted. He graduated from college, but hadn't worked very hard, which is probably what royals do. Good jobs were elusive in the Depression and then the war intervened. He literally turned his back on the real British royals during training exercises in Scotland; to him, the Irish Kings stood on a much higher plane than their British counterparts, who were an anathema. Twenty years after graduating from college my father finally got a steady executive job with the Post Office, including the all-important pension benefits which allowed him to retire at 57 and, in his view, live like a king.

The "Kings" myth was followed by another one which still rings in my ears. "We are just like the Kennedys." Well, we *were* Irish Catholics and avid Democrats, we lived in Massachusetts, and there were three sons in the family. But the resemblance ended there. Nonetheless, I thought seriously about politics; the royalty and Kennedy fantasies surely contributed to that. But in law school, the myths in my father's head (and in mine) ran into two headwinds which doomed my political career: I decided that the Vietnam War was not for me, despite my father's earlier efforts to convince me to join the Air Force ROTC; and I fell in love with and married a Jewish woman, which was viewed by him and probably everyone else in my Irish Catholic world as a complete repudiation of the faith. There was just no reconciling my abandonment of our royal and Kennedy lineage with the ordinary life of a lawyer I had chosen.

And even my successful legal career ran headlong into another axiom from my father rattling around in my head, this one in the form of a question: "When are you moving to Greenwich?" His son's large, beautiful home in Larchmont was not good enough for someone from New Haven who measured achievement by the ability to live in the most affluent part of Fairfield County.

My father has been dead for more than 15 years, but these phrases still resonate. No matter how successful I am, royalty, becoming a Kennedy and even Greenwich are beyond my grasp. But these dreams, like those of all immigrants, did propel me forward and I am grateful for that. Kingdoms, Kennedys and Connecticut Castles are not part of my vocabulary with my own three sons, which may be for the best. But I often wonder if the lack of these dreams has made their own lives much less interesting.

Chapter 6

LOATHSOME NICKNAMES

Why do some people, particularly parents, insist on giving their children nicknames? My name is John. My father's name was John. His father's name was John. I like my name just the way it is. But for some reason, throughout my childhood my parents insisted on calling me "Jackie," a nickname I loathe. And, of course, once I was branded with this name, its use multiplied among my many aunts, uncles, and cousins. I still hear it today, and cringe, more than 70 years after I was born.

There was no obvious need to give me this nickname. My father had the same name, but he was known as "Del." And my grandfather was already dead when I was born, so the question of redundancy was moot.

This nickname obsession also extended to my two younger brothers, who had perfectly respectable given names, Hugh and Dennis. Hugh was labeled "Jimmy" and Dennis was called "Den-Den." The three of us were "Jackie, Jimmy and Den-Den," which sounded like a traveling troupe of clowns.

Although there were other more compelling reasons for my later alienation, or more charitably, separation, from my family, this nickname fixation was certainly part of it. I did not want to be whoever they thought "Jackie" was. To this day, I insist that people use my given name, including my middle initial which stands for McDonald, my mother's maiden name. I also have to remind people all the time that my last name is spelled with an "e" not an "a" after the "l". My unadulterated name is a huge part of my identity and I don't like people messing around with it.

My wife, who was the victim of the moniker "Judykins," feels the same way I do about nicknames. We have tried to stamp them out in our family. Our sons are Matthew, Michael and Adam. We like their names, which is why we picked them, and resist the efforts by many people who should know better to mangle them. The most extreme case involved our son Adam. When he began playing soccer at age eight, someone on his team started calling him "Dilly." If Adam did not like this name, he wasn't going to say so, but Judy and I really hated it. We couldn't do much about this with his teammates, but we thought their parents would at least be willing to use our preferred name for him. As they say in Brooklyn, Fuhgeddaboutit! He was "Dilly" until he left for college and was finally able to reclaim his real name.

This nickname obsession did not stop with our children. When our oldest grandson was born, he was named MacLean, our daughter-in-law's maiden name. Our friends all insisted that he would be a "Mac" whether he or his parents or grandparents liked that handle or not. Fortunately, through our and our daughter-in-law's persistent objections, that nickname died in its infancy.

I know all of the above sounds very curmudgeonly, so I will end on a sweeter note. Our third grandson, born to our middle son and his wife, is named “Simeon Eroglu Delehanty”—a mouthful made up of Biblical, Turkish and Irish components. Our other grandchildren, perhaps not being able to get their mouths around this name, have rechristened him “Cinnamon Arugula.” Despite my disdain for nicknames, I must admit I love it.

Chapter 7

THE TAO OF HUGH

My brother Hugh's path to enlightenment began early, in the womb. He is three years, five months younger than me. Our father's plan was to have his children exactly four years apart so there would be no college tuition overlap. (That is the way Depression era men thought.). But Dad got frisky and Hugh emerged into the world seven months early. Seventy years later, he is still the guy who can't wait to embrace the world and everything in it.

Hugh almost did not make it beyond the age of two. Many two-year-olds get croup in the winter, but Hugh's case almost killed him. He was rushed to Yale New Haven Hospital in the middle of the night and was given an emergency tracheotomy. (He wears the scar on his throat to this day.) Hugh survived, but our parents John and Virginia were devastated and made Hugh's recovery the centerpiece of their lives.

I often crept by the darkened room where he slept after getting home from the hospital. Hugh spent weeks in a makeshift tent made from a card table, mosquito netting and a crude steaming device which looked like a tea kettle that never stopped whistling. If a two-year-old is able to self-reflect, as Hugh does so effortlessly now, this early cocoon was a great place to do it.

Hugh quickly made up for lost time when he emerged from the tent. He was a cute, curly headed bundle of energy with an infectious smile. This was a time when entertainment for young boys consisted primarily of getting a pack of baseball cards, chewing the slim piece of bubble gum inside, figuring out the value of the players depicted (Who is Wayne Terwilliger anyway?) and then getting rid of the unwelcome "doubles" to unsuspecting pals. That, Howdy Doody, and an ice cream cone was all we needed. Hugh took this process many steps further. He created whole worlds of what today would be called "fantasy teams" of players and spent hours having them play imaginary games. The cards and the men attached to them would fly all around the room, over the imaginary home run wall and touch all the bases. The poor pitchers were often neglected because there was very little excitement in a pitchers' duel. While I stacked my cards in piles with rubber bands, Hugh brought these little squares of cardboard to life and created his own baseball universe all over the living room floor. Our little brother Dennis got to pick them all up.

Hugh was a talented scrappy athlete in real life too. While I spent a lot of time daydreaming in right field, he was snagging balls in the infield and leading off the lineup. He was small for his age, but made up for it in energy and enthusiasm. His hair got curlier with sweat in the heat of the summer and he slept with his head on his fielder's mitt at night to make sure it stayed warm and remained supple.

While Hugh was Elvis, I was Pat Boone. Because of parental pressure on their first born and my own inclinations, I turned out to be the goody-goody nerd; Hugh got to be the cool, out of the box guy. In high school, he dated all the cute girls; I stayed home. In college Dad forced me to enroll in ROTC; Hugh got a pass. I finished college in four years; Hugh took five, including spending a half year in Greece with a girlfriend while Dad was paying for him to go to class. I went to law school; Hugh put some figurative flowers in his hair and went to San Francisco.

But I was a good stalking horse for Hugh. When I married Judy, a beautiful Jewish girl, all hell broke out in the Catholic Delehanty household. Dad boycotted the wedding and forced Mom to do the same. The feud lasted a very long time. But when Hugh married Barbara 16 years later, Dad had apparently learned his lesson about Jewish women; he was ecstatic that Hugh was settling down and he loved Barbara. He flew out to Pacific Heights and had a grand old time, hoisting one of his many Manhattans to celebrate.

Although we live very different lives and are three thousand miles apart, Hugh and I can pick up our next phone call just where we left off. He is so smart. We both love classic novels, which can be cool and nerdy at the same time. In one call, I mentioned that I was dipping into Tolstoy's *War and Peace.* Of course, Hugh knew the translator; he was reading her translation of *Anna Karenina.* And he also knew that Tolstoy was the first author to describe the intense internal emotional struggles of men at war.

Hugh is an accomplished writer whose work is widely known. He is the author of *Sacred Hoops*, *Eleven Rings,* and *Caring for Your Parents.* Formerly the editor in chief of AARP publications, he is also a contributor to Sports Illustrated, People, Mindfulness and other magazines. All of Hugh's writings appear to flow seamlessly out of the boy who emerged from weeks in the tent and created an imaginary world populated by Duke Snider and Willy Mays. I will never appreciate poetry slams or electronic cellos with no strings like they play in San Rafael, but I love having a brother who does.

Hugh is not only a wonderful brother; he is a great son. When Dad was succumbing to Parkinson's, we divided responsibilities three ways: I handled the finances; our youngest brother Dennis handled Dad's move to assisted living; and Hugh handled the most important part, making sure Dad had the emotional and medical support he needed at the end of his life. No one could have done it better than Hugh.

Chapter 8.

THE EVOLUTION OF "DEN-DEN"

My two younger brothers and I were known to my parents as Jimmy, Den-Den, and Jackie (a name I loathe). Our real names are Hugh, Dennis, and John. Although our parents and pet names are long gone, the infantile stigma of these names still reverberates, and Den-Den's name is particularly symbolic of the distance he and I experienced in the early parts of our lives.

My siblings and I were supposed to be born four years apart so that we would not overlap in college and force our parents to pay more than one tuition at a time. I am sure this was on John and Virginia's minds when they got around to having sex. They jumped the gun with Hugh, who was born only three years after me. I had to fix that problem by skipping the third grade, restoring the four-year gap that was the plan.

Although I have a crystal-clear memory of my own boyhood in Hamden Connecticut and a bit of Hugh's part in it, I have no solid memories of Dennis, who is seven years younger. There are at least two reasons for that. John, and to some extent Virginia, had big plans for me. In his delusions, often fed by alcohol, Dad thought that I could be the start of a dynasty, a mini-version of the Kennedys. I was precocious, which fed the narrative, and my brothers, particularly Dennis, were left in the dust.

The second reason is that, regrettably, I paid little or no attention to Dennis as he was growing up. That seven-year gap was huge, at least for me. The problem was exacerbated when we moved to Weymouth, Massachusetts when I was twelve and Dennis was five. I hated being ripped from the home where I had grown up in Connecticut, which was within striking distance of the glories of New York City, and dropped into a blue-collar suburb of Boston, where my classmates told crude jokes in funny accents.

Dennis thrived in Weymouth and almost immediately adopted the local accent. I got out of town when I was 16 and went to Brown University, 40 miles and many light years away from Weymouth. No one would ever know from speaking with me that I had grown up in Massachusetts.

Hugh also went to Brown, four years after I did, although he took a detour to Greece with a girlfriend half way through. This upset the four-year clock and made my father furious. Cracks in the dynasty plans began to appear.

Then the dynasty crumbled. After Brown, I went to the University of Chicago Law School. Law school was surely consistent with my father's plan. But he did not count on my meeting and falling in love with Judy, a student at Chicago's Graduate School of Social Work who also happened to be Jewish and from New Jersey. All hell broke loose in Weymouth when my father found out about our plans to marry. He did everything he could to stop us—writing vitriolic letters; hauling me off to the Monsignor, a closeted gay family friend; and threatening to boycott the wedding.

Dennis, the only one of us still living at home, had to endure the wrath my father aimed at me. He may have been torn but appeared to side with Dad; he really didn't have a choice. The conflagration in Weymouth clearly affected him. He began smoking marijuana and his grades suffered. Brown was not a possibility for him, as it had been for Hugh and me. He enrolled at the University of Denver, and later transferred to Colby College in Maine.

After graduation from Chicago, Judy and I were VISTA volunteers in DC. Dennis visited us there. His loyalties still appeared to be with John and Virginia, from whom we were now estranged. We attended his college graduation, which was awkward for all concerned, and did not see Dennis again for more than four years.

Our reunion was prompted by a family crisis. Mom was diagnosed with glioblastoma, an incurable brain tumor, the same disease that killed Teddy Kennedy. I was in New York. Our son Matthew was two and Judy was pregnant with Michael. Hugh was in California. Dennis was in Moscow, learning Russian at the Pushkin Institute. Dad expected all of us to come to Weymouth for the duration of Mom's illness and help him care for her, an impossible demand. He ultimately tore her away from Weymouth and the world she knew and moved her to live with her sister in Annapolis Maryland. He refused to hire any professional help.

Dennis volunteered to assist with Mom's care as soon as he returned from Russia. He became the golden boy, unlike Hugh and me who only made occasional visits and were roundly criticized for our apparent indifference. Consciously or unconsciously, Dennis cemented his relationship with Dad, which later became very important. Dad helped Dennis get an executive position in the Postal Service of which Dad was an alumnus. All three of us had been mail carriers in college so we jokingly referred to the Post Office as the "family business."

Dennis married Elizabeth in Venezuela and was transferred to the Universal Postal Union in Switzerland where their daughter Carmen was born. They returned to DC in the early '90s. Dennis thrived as an executive in the Postal Service and later the State Department. He negotiated postal treaties around the world and became fluent in Russian, Mandarin, Spanish, French and Italian.

The trust he developed with Dad during my mother's illness and death was invaluable when Dad himself became ill with Parkinson's. Unlike the recriminations surrounding Mom's death, Hugh, Dennis and I seamlessly paved the way to Dad's ultimate demise. I handled legal and financial issues, like Dad's safe deposit box stuffed with stock certificates; Hugh handled medical issues; and Dennis orchestrated the hardest part of all, persuading Dad to leave the home that was falling down around him in Weymouth, with Mom's clothes still in the closets, and move to assisted living and then to a nursing home.

The bond that we brothers struck during that time has endured and, although we are separated geographically, we communicate almost daily. The seven-year gap between Dennis and me has disappeared.

Dennis has retired and now lives in Lake Nona, a fascinating new community outside of Orlando, where all the streets are named after Nobel laureates. Every month Dennis writes a profile of one of them for the Lake Nona paper. His pieces are very well written and provide a blend of the Nobelists' professional accomplishments and their relation to the people who live in Lake Nona.

Last summer we celebrated Dennis's 70th birthday in Ireland, with a host of relatives near and far. Dad would be happy about that. Despite the storms that he created and we all endured, I am very fortunate to still have Jimmy and Den-Den in my life.

Chapter 9

THE FAMILY SECRET RIGHT IN FRONT OF YOUR NOSE

Some families hide their secrets very well. In others, the secret is out in the open, but no one in the family seems to know. It takes an outsider to point out the obvious.

My father drank. But his drinking was just part of the family landscape; it was taken for granted and no one paid much attention to it. "I ate a large lunch at the office" was his usual refrain when he walked in the door at 6 pm. So my mother, two brothers and I ate our dinners while Dad drank a 32 ounce bottle of Schaefer beer right from the fridge, conveniently located behind his chair. Sometimes he drank two.

After dinner he would take a nap while Mom ironed or corrected her second-grade class papers and my brothers and I did our homework, always on our own. Dad would get up at midnight and read until 2 or 3 in the morning. He said he was "guarding the house," although his watchfulness was always accompanied by a bottle of Irish whiskey.

After a few hours of sleep, he was up bright and early with Mom, ate his poached egg and went to work. At 6 pm the evening routine started all over again.

Dad did not jog, golf, play tennis or swim. His favorite weekend activity was hanging out at the local "gin mill." This term originated during Prohibition when my grandfather made gin in the bathtub, presiding over his own "gin mill." On rare occasions, Dad would take the family for pizza (and beer for him) at his usual hangout; joining him there always made it an awkward night for all of us.

My mother came from a very large family in New Haven. Every Christmas, after Mass, we drove three hours from our home outside Boston to my grandmother's two-bedroom cottage there. The tiny living room was filled, wall to wall, with aunts, uncles, cousins, boxes, ribbons, and great swaths of wrapping paper.

The McDonalds, including my mother's brothers, were teetotalers; there was no liquor in the house. Dad and my Polish uncle, Joe, who was married to my mother's sister, always managed to slip out for the night and find a happy hour—or three. We did not see them again until the morning.

If anyone noticed my father's absence, it was ascribed to his Irish Catholic ancestry. The Protestant McDonalds assumed that Irish people always behaved that way. It went with the red splotchy complexion and the belief that leprechauns were real.

When my wife and I got engaged, my father flew into a rage. He admired and respected Jews but it was the ultimate betrayal for me to marry one. He wrote me daily diatribes, often ten pages at a time—in capital letters—on how I had betrayed my heritage for which his ancestors had fought and died. Although I did not know it at the time, most of the letters were probably written when Dad was drinking and "guarding the house."

Over time, Dad calmed down somewhat and the vitriolic letters stopped. On Judy's and my rare visits, he was always in the same seat in front of the fridge with a large bottle of beer within close reach. Once he and my mother came to visit Judy's parents in New Jersey, an unusual venture for him outside of Weymouth. As we said good night to him and my mother, Dad pulled from the trunk of his car a gallon of Manhattans.

It never even occurred to me that Dad was an alcoholic. He held a steady job, supported the family (with help from my mother's income as a teacher), read voraciously, was an avid student of politics and a highly intelligent, college educated man. And he never raised a hand to us.

My eyes didn't open until years after he died. We knew another man who ran a marina near our house on the Cape. He was surly, mean and unfriendly. Then he changed, and became almost pleasant. "What happened?" we asked one of his workers. The answer was simple: "He stopped drinking."

That was a revelation. It explained the nasty letters, the aloofness, the rage, the paranoia. My father was a captive of his addiction to alcohol and I completely missed it. It is too late to forgive him now, but the thought of who he might have been without the drink haunts me to this day.

Chapter 10

MY FATHER'S CLASSIC BOOKS

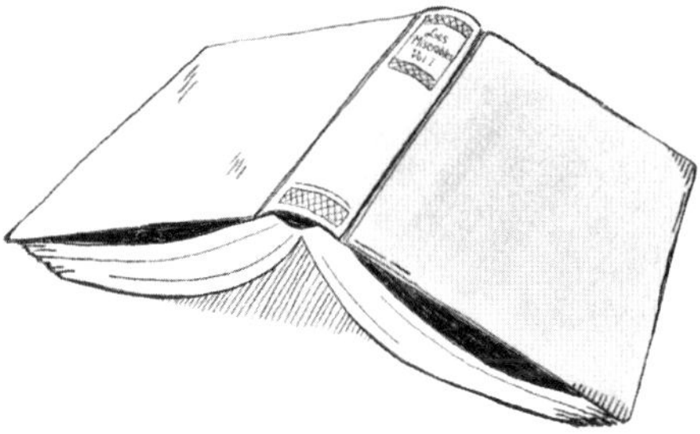

Every few months a large box arrives at my house from London. In it is one or more beautifully bound and illustrated classic books from The Folio Society. Each book is lovingly wrapped in insulated plastic (the stuff that pops when you squeeze it) and accompanied by a note "Your books were packed by Emma." *Mansfield Park* by Jane Austen arrived just yesterday.

The books are expensive, often very long, and take up lots of real estate on my bookshelves, which groan from their weight. Although I have read many of them, it is very difficult to keep up. I am not sure I will ever get through Winston Churchill's six-volume history of the Second World War. Fortunately, I have a second home in Naples, Florida, where I can house some of the books that can't fit in New Rochelle.

Why am I compelled to keep adding these books to my already overgrown library? The answer to that question goes back to April 1946, the year after I was born. My parents and I lived in a tiny four room cottage with one bathroom outside of New Haven, Connecticut. Although the post-war period is often called the beginning of America's boom, that wasn't the case for my father. Although he was a college graduate, a Captain in the Army during the war in Europe, and a very bright man, he was stuck in a low paying blue collar job, which it took him many years to escape.

We had no car, no TV, and barely any furniture. The one luxury we had was my parents' collection of books from a publishing company called Heritage Press. Heritage published the world's best literature in stunning volumes, profusely illustrated and always accompanied by a light green pamphlet. The pamphlet did not focus on the content of the book, but rather on how it was made, the choice of the typeface and paper, the binding, the provenance of the illustrator, and all of the features that made the book a work of art. My mother would inscribe each book with my father's name and the date they acquired it. She then added a bookplate labeled "Ex Libris The Delehantys."

My father was an alcoholic and verbally abusive, but he was extraordinarily well read. He would pore over these books well into the early morning hours and entertain me and later my brothers with rollicking tales from *The Three Musketeers*, *Les Miserables*, *The Odyssey*, the Brothers Grimm and many others. He even told stories from less well-known books like the *Arabian Nights* and the *Rubaiyat of Omar Khayyam.*

As soon as I could read myself, I would pull some of these books from the shelves, take them out of their slipcases, admire the drawings and try to make my way through some of the text. When I had to write a book report for school, I could read my father's edition of *Oliver Twist* rather than going to the library; the illustrations of Fagin and Bill Sykes were even more frightening than Dickens' own vivid descriptions. And I loved reading the Grimm Brothers' tales, the gorier the better. As I grew older, I would even dip into some of Montaigne's essays, something I would never have done if these books were not sitting in our living room and I had nothing better to do.

When I was seven, my favorite aunt gave me a hardback version of *Penrod*, by Booth Tarkington. It was the beginning of my own library. In retrospect, I was flattered that she thought I could read it, but she may have known about my early infatuation with the books in our house.

After I left home and went to college and law school, my relationship with my father became very stormy. The fact that I had married a Jew and abandoned the Catholic Church was an affront to his overly developed emotional connection with Irish history. Our feud lasted 30 years. We only reconciled in the last year of his life following his long battle with Parkinson's disease. After his death, my brothers and I divided the Heritage books. I have all one thousand pages of *Les Miserables* (dated and signed by my mother in April 1946), the *Oliver Twist* from my book report days, and many others. My brothers have the rest.

Since my father died, I have added to the collection, sometimes at a furious pace. Heritage no longer exists, but I found its successor, The Folio Society, in England, where they still take the production of beautiful books seriously. I have continued the tradition started by my parents to buy and collect them. All of the Greeks and Romans are accounted for, as well as every Victorian novelist, scores of English mystery writers, and even Fitzgerald, Faulkner and Hemingway.

These books, even the newer ones, are a constant reminder to me of the gift my parents gave me by filling their home with exceptional literature. They bind me to my past and soften my recollection of it. And they represent values that I share with my brothers who are fortunate to have their own collections of our parents' books, a fact we often discuss. I hope that my own children and grandchildren will one day appreciate the huge role that these books have played in our family's history.

They are also for me a safe refuge in an increasingly chaotic world. Reading Trollope is a wonderful antidote to the news. As I write this, many of them are sitting on the shelves by the side of my desk, in multiple colors, shapes and sizes, from Austen to Zola and scores of other writers in between. But there are still many gaps to fill. I can't wait for the next package from my unseen Folio Society friend, Emma.

Chapter 11

ATOP THE CHOKECHERRY TREE

From the top of the chokecherry tree in the yard next door I could see my whole world. It seemed that the tree had grown there just for me. No one ever plants a chokecherry tree. Why would you? The fruit is like a tiny plum the size of the tip of a small finger and 90 percent pit. And the trees are not very attractive or large. But mine was special: it was 20 feet tall with branches perfectly spaced for my 8-year-old legs. Munching on the fruit and spitting out the pits was an added bonus in my perch way above the ground below.

I loved everything I saw from up there. My tiny Cape Cod house on a postage stamp lot where I lived with my parents and 4-year-old brother Hugh. The forty little identical houses on both sides of my street all in a row. The myriad vendors who came by every day, some with horses pulling their wares: the ragman calling "Cash paid for rags"; the knife sharpener; the milk and butter man; the grocery van; and of course, the Good Humor man. All of them, with their clanging bells, sing-song patter, and brightly painted carts brought the exciting outside world to our carless block.

Behind my house was the cemetery, surrounded by a six-foot-high chain link fence. Nothing could keep me and my friends away. We reached the other side by making holes like groundhogs under the fence. The gravestones and whoever lay beneath them did not bother us; the many stones were perfect hiding places for our games of hide and seek. And the grassy area in the back of the cemetery, where no one had yet been buried, was an ideal field for touch football.

Our own backyard reflected my parents' post-War sensibilities. They grew red, white and blue grapes in an arbor next to the Victory Garden, which they still maintained long after VE and VJ Day. The tomato crop fed most of the neighborhood when it arrived, seemingly all at once. Our backyard was also the site of home plate for our nightly baseball games. None of the 50-foot-wide yards was large enough for a field, so we used four of them. The catcher squatted and the batter stood in our yard, the pitcher and the infield were in the next yard and the outfield was in a third. A home run landed in the fourth. Running the bases was like clearing hurdles in a track race because there were bushes or low fences dividing each yard. Sometimes we would play in the street, but dodging the cars presented its own challenges.

Just below the tree in the third yard was my hiding place next to our neighbor's garage, the only one on the block. There I hid for hours when my parents came after me for hitting a girl with a rock. I surrendered after it got dark and went to bed without dinner, but I never told them about my refuge. I could have used it when my father stormed after me for calling Patricia Hollander a "JB." I didn't even know what it meant, but came up with Jewish Bagel, something I had heard of but never tasted. Dad was not amused. The war was still fresh in his veteran's mind and he would not tolerate my bigotry, no matter how innocent it may have been.

Across the street I could see our neighbor's bocce court, which he had lovingly carved from the red Connecticut clay on which all of our houses stood. It may have helped him overcome his homesickness for Italy. Sadly, but understandably, he wouldn't let us play on it, so we made our own, in Butchy Iacobellis's backyard, with a little pink ball for the pill and softballs for the bocce balls. Mrs. Iacobellis occasionally peeked out the window at us, but she spent almost every hour of the day inside making Italian "gravy." I always wished she would bring some over to our house. It would certainly moisten the pot roast which Mom cooked for hours in the pressure cooker.

Behind Butchy's house was the farm, a throwback to the time before our street and many like it erased much of the countryside north of New Haven. Crossing the farm was the shortest way to get to school, particularly useful if we were late. But rumor had it that the farmer had a shotgun and a disposition like Peter Rabbit's Mr. McGregor. I never got shot, because most of the time I took the long way around. Nonetheless, the risk, whether imagined or real, made the trip to school much more interesting.

The farm was also the place where the older boys went to smoke and gawk at Playboy magazine. One day they left one behind and I saw a photo (now very famous) of Marilyn Monroe spread out on a red blanket in all her glory. I was transfixed. I did not know who she was but I worshipped her nonetheless. I hid the magazine in a hollowed-out tree and visited Marilyn every day until she and the magazine got caught in a downpour and were ruined.

A few houses down from us and barely visible from my tree was Mrs. Robitsky's house. She had two huge purple beech trees in her tiny front yard on which she hung 20 or more bird feeders. Her yard was a mecca for hundreds of birds. Mrs. Robitsky spoke with an accent and always wore black. She was a little scary, particularly on Halloween. But the birds loved her and had no fear. They would take sunflower seeds straight from between her lips. I do not know where Mrs. Robitsky came from, but she and the birds brought a sense of peace and adventure to our block.

Although my world was narrow, it was idyllic, at least to my very young eyes. I know I cannot trade it for the complicated one I live in now, but spending the time to recreate it in this piece and reliving my innocent childhood brings me great joy.

Chapter 12

EATING AT MOM'S

A friend and I were having lunch the other day. She had piled her salad high with beets. She offered me one. "No thanks," I said; I hated beets and never ate them.

When I was young, I was forced to eat canned beets two or three times a week. They were a focal point of Mom's post-war cuisine, allegedly because they were filled with iron or some other life-saving mineral. This conversation brought back a flood of memories of the terrible foods I was forced to eat at Mom's, the only culinary option I had. It is a miracle that I survived.

Mom had an aversion to red meat, but brown and gray were fine. Almost every night she brought out the pressure cooker, a frightening instrument in itself, with the possibility of an explosion any minute. This sealed pot, with its little dial dangling at the top, was supposed to cook the pot roast, wound up in strings, in a few minutes. But Mom did not trust it. So she let the meat cook long enough to make the blood and any other nutrients vanish. The resulting slices could just as easily have been used to make a pair of shoes as they could a meal.

Mom was obsessed with cans. If we lost our can opener we would all starve. Everything came out of a can: peas, beans, corn, the aforementioned beets and even fruit, pineapple rings and the ubiquitous fruit cup, with little chunks of pears and peaches which had nestled in the can for months.

They say that bread is the staff of life, but Mr. Wonder had a different idea. He found a way to discard all of the grains and other nutrients and create a pure white loaf consisting mainly of air. It was difficult to resist the festive red, blue and yellow balls on the package, but the product itself rendered sandwich making a challenge; a knife full of peanut butter went right through the bread and into the counter. Maybe that's why Mom made me cream cheese and olive sandwiches for lunch every day.

If Mom wanted to try more international fare, there were also cans for that. Who can forget the great Italian chef de cuisine, Mr. Boyardee, who suspended little pasta circles and tiny meatballs in a glutinous orange sauce with a sodium level that could cause a stroke on the spot. Even more exotic was Mr. Chun King, who also satisfied Mom's craving for cans. His chow mein came in THREE cans stacked one on top of the other: the chicken and gravy at the bottom; the vegetables, including water chestnuts, which were as far from our usual fare as we were from China, in the middle; and the best part, the crispy noodles, at the top. In light of the alternatives, I could eat chow mein every night.

One of those alternatives that did not come in a can was liver. Mom was convinced that my brothers and I needed iron, so once a week was liver night. It is almost impossible to conceal the offal-like taste or strange texture of this stuff. Mom cooked it with onions which didn't really help and she never offered to add bacon probably because we would have eaten that and left the liver alone.

Another respite from the liver night also came from a can, in fact a whole row of cans labeled "Campbells." On Sunday nights we slurped tomato soup sprinkled with popcorn while we watched "Lassie." Other nights Mom would pour Campbell's soup—mushroom, vegetable, onion—on top of whatever she was cooking, to give the meal a little pizzazz. I carried on this legacy. When I graduated from college and had my own place, the ONLY dish I made every night was browned hamburger meat smothered in Campbell's vegetable soup.

What did we wash down Mom's offerings with? Bottles of whole milk, of course, delivered by the milk man every day, with two inches of cream at the top—the best part. Actually, almost everything was delivered to our house in the suburbs of New Haven. Every day at 5 o'clock, a truck would come by on our street ringing its bell. Mom and the other moms would stream out to buy their cans. We had no car, so this truck was our food lifeline.

Mom was a woman of her time. Her food options were very limited and she relied heavily on the post-war buzz about what was the best thing to serve her family. And although the food sounded and in fact was awful, Mom had one talent that transcended it all. She was a fabulous pie baker: apple, pumpkin, peach, you name it, with a light thin crust and always served a la mode. I wished that I could live on pie alone.

Chapter 13

PASS THE POT ROAST

They say it's a good thing for parents to eat with their children every night, and that may be true. In our atomized, electronic world, family dinners seem like a relic and many bemoan their apparent decline. But having spent at least 18 years of my early life around the family dinner table, I wonder if it was as benign as those rose-colored glasses make it appear.

Take 1958. I was 13, in junior high school, living in a tiny Cape Cod style house in South Weymouth, Massachusetts. Dinner was at six and always in the kitchen. (The dining room was used only three times a year: Easter, Thanksgiving and Christmas.) The kitchen was the nerve center of the house; in addition to being the place where food and drink were consumed, it was where the bills were paid, newspapers, magazines and books read, clothes ironed, important decisions made and family squabbles erupted and occasionally settled. Other than their bedroom, my parents hardly went elsewhere in the house. Like their own working-class parents, they did not feel very comfortable in what they called the "parlor."

There were five of us and we always sat in the same seats around the rectangular kitchen table. Father, that's what we called him (he was not really the "Dad" type), sat at the head of the table in front of the fridge where he kept his quarts of Schaefer beer. I sat at the other end, as far away from him as possible. Mom sat between us on my left, and my two younger brothers, who were 10 and 6, sat across from her on my right. Father, my mom and I formed a triangle where all the action was. I can barely recall my brothers' presence, let alone what they said.

The food was typical for that time, plentiful, caloric and overcooked. The pot roast, held together with packaging string, was cooked in a pressure cooker until it was just this side of gray. The green beans and corn were straight from the Libby's cans. The potatoes were the stars of the show and appeared every night, mashed with butter and cream, baked with butter and cheese or roasted with lots of oil. Dessert was Jell-O or, on special occasions, ice cream: vanilla, chocolate and strawberry in alternating layers. Although not much of a cook, Mom could bake and there were often macaroons and peanut butter cookies on the table.

Father didn't eat any of it.

Every night at 6 pm, as soon he arrived at the door, he told Mom he had had a big lunch in Boston and wasn't hungry, a rejection she bore with a shrug. But he did sit with us and poured out his bottomless quart of beer while we ate. And then he held forth on the family orthodoxy: We were Democrats engaged in a holy war with the loathsome Republican plutocrats; we were Irish, directly descended from the Kings of Ireland; we were Catholics (even though Mom was a Methodist and Father hardly ever set foot in a church); and finally, we were the children of survivors of the Depression and World War II and should never forget the hardships our parents went through to bring us into the world.

Mom did not question any of this, even though she undoubtedly had her own views. Nonetheless, she was tasked with putting our family ideology into action, something Father was too lazy, timid, or stupefied to do. She posted the election signs for the Democrats, enlisting me to help. She brought us to Church every Sunday, even though she did not belong. She fostered all the Irish myths, sublimating her own New England Yankee roots. As a school teacher in our local school, she knew how to manage.

And where was I, the third corner of the dinner triangle? As the heir apparent to the family name (the laws of primogeniture still applied in South Weymouth), I was supposed to be the next JFK, although I would have to make do without a family fortune. Over the pot roast and potatoes, the themes were drilled into me: Get all A's, serve the Mass, join the Scouts, carry the flag, hang Democratic signs on all the doorknobs, prepare for the next phase of the family's greatness. I never dissented. Mom was a silent partner in this one-way conversation directed at me. But I could see the expression on her face change from disappointment to hope as it swung between her flawed husband and her precocious son. This triangle at the family dinner table became the template for the rest of our lives together, as firmly bound as the string around the pot roast.

Chapter 14

WHO NEEDS THIRD GRADE, ANYWAY?

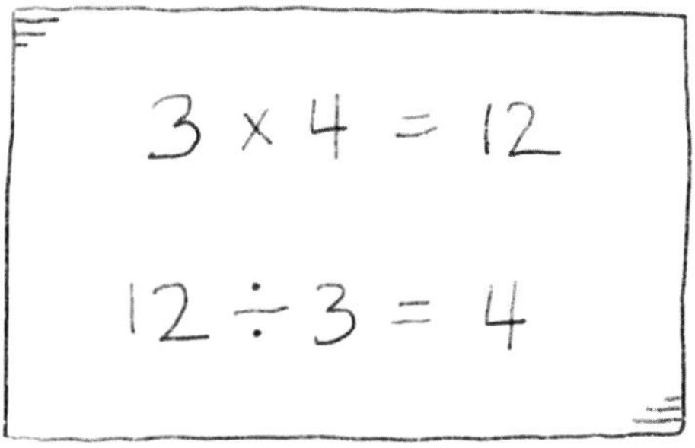

I reached my intellectual peak at age seven, and have spent the rest of my life trying to climb back up to the top of that mountain.

My pre-K years are almost a blur. I spent them with my Mom and later my little brother Hugh. I can't remember being particularly stimulated. Mom gave me a few toys and left me to my own devices. My socialization consisted of playing cowboys and Indians. I was Hopalong Cassidy; he and his posse always won. The high points of my pre-K years were taking the trolley into downtown New Haven with my Mom and picking out some penny candy at the department store counter. That's it.

Kindergarten was more of the same; except now I spent my days in the big brick schoolhouse around the corner from our street. Mom dropped me off on day one and never set foot in the building again. She was not indifferent; she and the other mothers saw no reason to hang around; that's what Miss Kindt was for. So she stayed home and kept her eye on baby Hugh. I walked home by myself for tomato soup and tuna fish at lunch. Then it was back to the blocks, piling one on top of the other and knocking them down. The little girls did not like that, but for the other boys and me, it was just what we did. I could not read or write and my social skills were embryonic, but I did manage to make it to the first grade.

Miss Hickey gave me my first book and told me to read it. Dick, Jane and Spot may not have led the most interesting lives, but the process of reading about them was fascinating to me and much better than piling up those blocks. I quickly learned that there were books about people other than Dick and Jane: George Washington, Abraham Lincoln, Thomas Edison, Horton the Elephant, Thidwick the Big-Hearted Moose. I was okay at baseball, but really good at reading, so I spent much of my time at the library, hauling home and devouring piles of books.

In Miss Horn's second grade, I figured out that I could write as well as read. Cursive was a pain. Putting the steel nib in the black pen holder, dipping it into the inkwell on my desk and trying not to spill ink all over my white shirt was a challenge every day. I still can't do it to this day even with a ball point pen. Thank God someone invented the pencil. A pencil just had to be sharpened from time to time and never spilled any ink. And I could use it to print, a much easier way to put my thoughts down on paper than that accursed cursive.

I wrote my autobiography through age seven with my pencil. Believe it or not, this story was much more graphic and compelling than the four paragraphs above. It had the immediacy of recent memory. Miss Horn was blown away by the fact that she had a prodigy in her midst. She asked me to read my life story to the whole class; they all applauded. She then had copies mimeographed for everyone to bring home. To my parents' delight, the adulation and the A's kept piling up.

Then I peaked. On the first day of third grade, the principal came to class and took Jill Teitelman and me to her office. She told us that we did not have to go to the third grade. We could skip it entirely and go on to fourth. She showed us how to multiply and divide in a few minutes and said that was all we had to know about third grade. There wasn't any discussion with my parents about whether skipping was a good idea; my mother had skipped third grade also, so maybe they thought this was something our family just did; it was in our genes. They were also pleased that the principal thought Jackie was so smart. Yes, the two of us who skipped were Jackie and Jill.

From fourth grade on the glory days were over. I was no longer the boy genius, just the shortest guy in the class who always stood at the front of the line because it was arranged by height. The A's continued, but I got C's in conduct and effort. I had a miniscule attention span and always relied on my intuition rather than doing my homework. It had worked in second grade, why not for the rest of my school career? Being short and small was not a good combination on the Wednesday walks from school to church for catechism with the nuns. The other 4th grade guys loved to pin me on the ground and make me eat grass.

When I was in the eighth grade we moved. I was just 12. The boys in the new school were huge and hairy and had all gone through puberty. They were obsessed with sex. They bragged about their night dreams, both the spontaneous kind and the ones they brought on themselves. Every time someone mentioned the number 69 they snickered. I had no idea what they were talking about. I was virtually hairless, still short, serving as an altar boy, and infatuated with Jesus. Puberty was light years away.

Not surprisingly, high school was a social disaster. The girls were just as sexually precocious and physically developed as the guys. But I had barely grown an inch and did not even have peach fuzz on my cheeks. And I spent most of my time playing cards with my equally nerdy friends. I never had the courage to ask a girl out and missed both of the proms, a loss I regret to this day.

Then began my life of almosts.

I almost got into the college I wanted. I almost graduated cum laude. I almost made the Law Review. I almost made partner at the law firm. But that second-grade blaze of glory, when I was the very best, never happened again.

More than sixty years later I am still trying to get back to the top of the mountain. My trial lawyer days are over. But, even as a mediator I have to be the best and settle the case even if the parties don't really want to. In my memoir class, I want to write the best piece and have everyone applaud when I finish reading, just like in second grade.

I have had a wonderful professional and personal life, one that many would envy. But I often wonder how it would have turned out if the principal had just left me in the third grade. If anyone had asked me, which of course they didn't, I would have said: "I'd like to stay right where I am."

Chapter 15

MY UNSHEDDABLE SKIN

I am the descendant of generations of Scots and Irish who spent most of their days mucking about in peat bogs under leaden skies. Although the sun might have peeked out for a minute or two, most of the time the air was filled (or kissed, depending on your point of view) with a gentle rain.

As a result of this lack of sun for thousands of years, my ancestors bequeathed to me their defining genetic characteristics, lily white skin, almost transparent blue eyes and, at least when I was born, albino-like blond hair. I came into this world as white as a mushroom popping up in the dark.

Later the freckles arrived; I was called "freckle face," a term of endearment I hated. But there they were, little blotches all over my body which made me look like a tiny giraffe. Little did I know then that each of these little patches of brown was a ticking time bomb which ultimately made my dermatologist very rich.

Every summer my skin was burned to a crisp because I stayed out in the sun too long. Mom covered me with gobs of Calamine lotion to ease the pain. I loved the pink color and sweet smell of this stuff, and the fact that it saved me from my self-inflicted wounds. It might have been easier to put on suntan lotion before I went out to play, but this was the '50s and we were either not smart enough to know about that—or more likely, Coppertone just cost too much to buy.

The burns did not stop me from wanting to have a tan. I grew up with many kids whose ancestors came from the Mediterranean. They all had rich brown skin. Although it was futile, I wanted to look like all of them. One day I bought a big bottle of a new product called QT which guaranteed a tan even for hopelessly white people like me. I slathered it over my body one night and waited for the results. When I went down for breakfast, my Mom saw me and almost fainted. QT's version of a tan was bright orange, a color which covered my entire body and lingered for weeks.

I was not attracted to girls who had skin like mine. I married Judy who loved the sun and had beautiful tanned skin. Fortunately, the QT had worn off when I met her. I loved being with Judy at the beach, but I had finally learned that, what for her was a place to luxuriate, was for me a battleground. I armed myself with bottles of 60 SPF lotion, a long-sleeved shirt, a wide-brimmed hat and a huge umbrella. But still the sun caught up with me on my sprint from the blanket to the ocean. When Judy asked me to take her to the Caribbean, I took special precautions; I bought a full-length caftan with a hood. Wearing it, I looked like a sheik wandering around the outskirts of Riyadh.

Seventeen years ago, I had a kidney transplant, a procedure that saved my life. (This was caused by another genetic inheritance from my Scottish side, a tale for another day.). My nephrologist said there would be no side effects, save one. The immunosuppressive drugs would make my already vulnerable skin susceptible to all sorts of conditions ending in the sound “oma”: basal cell carcinoma, squamous cell carcinoma, and the big one, melanoma.

Mr. Basal and Mr. Squamous are regular visitors, but so far Mr. Melanoma has stayed away. Every few months, my dermatologist freezes, scrapes, cuts and otherwise obliterates these growths on my skin which pop up like the aforementioned mushrooms. Every once in a while, he does something called a MOHS surgery where he removes layer after layer until he is happy that all the bad cells are gone. He once took six layers off the top of my ear, which he said was a record. I had to hire a plastic surgeon to restore my ear to its lovely pre-MOHS shape.

There are other ways to ward off these “omas”; none of them are much fun. I have stood in a booth with goggles on while light beams shoot at my face for ten minutes, turning it bright red and supposedly killing off the cells that may go bad. I have applied a powerful cream every night for weeks that does the same thing. Going to work with crimson splotches all over my face is mortifying. Fortunately, Judy has a cornucopia of makeup. She skillfully applies some opaque skin colored stuff to my face which makes me look almost normal again.

I have never particularly identified with any other creature in the animal kingdom. But you can understand why, every once in a while, I think about our friend the snake. He does not have to see the dermatologist every three months. When his skin gets scruffy and all banged up he just sheds it and gets a new one. I would not like to crawl around on my belly, but I sure would love to shed my otherwise unsheddable skin.

Chapter 16

ESCAPING WEYMOUTH, THE NERD'S REVENGE

I was always an outsider in high school. I moved to Weymouth, Massachusetts in 8th grade, leaving behind a diverse, affluent town in Connecticut where I had grown up. Weymouth was mostly blue collar, 75% Catholic, 25% Protestant and 100% white. There was not a Black face or a Jew among the 50,000 people in town.

I was small, short and young. I had skipped the 3rd grade, so I was 13 when I started high school and 16 when I finished. I didn't shave until I got to college. I was clueless about sex and did not know why the number "69" was so titillating. I could barely speak to a girl, let alone date one. I did not go to the junior or the senior prom. I had my first date and my first kiss well after I graduated. I had a few guy friends; they were nerds like me, although the word had not yet been invented. We played cards and hung out, trying to figure out how we ended up on the outside.

Like most high schools, the jocks and the cheerleaders were the people who mattered. They were handsome and beautiful. The guys were muscular with packs of cigarettes rolled up in their t-shirt sleeves. And the girls had cute faces and nice breasts. The boys drove muscle cars and convertibles like the kids in "Grease" and raced around town at night with six-packs readily available in the rear seats where much of the action took place. Half the guys and many of the girls were in what was called vocational school, where they learned to be mechanics and secretaries, well regarded callings in those days. We college-bound kids called them "Vokies" behind their backs.

The town refused to build a second high school, which it desperately needed. Why? Because it did not want to break up the football team. That meant double sessions: 1 pm to 4 pm for 10th grade, and 8 am to noon for 11th and 12th. It is amazing that we learned anything. The rest of the time I was home alone. I had a crush on my piano teacher, which helped to pass the time (I was awful) and made my lunch, usually a pizza from scratch. And I spent a lot of time on my knees in church.

At the time, I thought I wanted to be a part of all of this exciting and glamorous high school life, if I could just find a way in. But it never happened. Instead, I took courses that steered me to college, Latin, French, Math, Social Studies, Science, English. I was a voracious reader, but an indifferent student. I got A's because: a) I was good at school; and b) I feared my parents, who expected me to go to Yale. They had grown up in New Haven; Yale, with its gothic architecture and manicured lawns, was the paragon of achievement for them. And I was very good at standardized tests. I have no idea why, but my SAT scores made me Ivy League material, and they started me on the long road out of Weymouth.

As it turned out, Yale would not have me. So I went to Brown, 20 miles down the road from home. And there I saw a world beyond Weymouth. My roommate was an affluent Jewish guy from New Jersey. He sent his clothes home to be laundered and sent back by the two maids who lived there. His Dad would regularly send him clothes from Tripler's in New York. And he had his own convertible and phone. He was a nerd as well, but a rich one which made nerdiness a little more tolerable. I began to see that the world beyond Weymouth had real possibilities.

Many of the social stigmas I had in high school carried over to college. I was still small, short and young, but the world was opening up a bit and by senior year I had a real girlfriend, an accomplishment which vastly outweighed my achievements in class. But the Educational Testing Service saved me again. My Law School Admission Test score was excellent. I could go just about anywhere, except Yale. I chose the University of Chicago because they gave me a free three-year ride. I had never been west of the Hudson and had never been on an airplane. Weymouth began to appear much more remote.

Then two things happened. I did not cause them to happen, but they changed my life and really put Weymouth in the back mirror. I met Judy, a beautiful girl from New Jersey who was a graduate student in social work. Not long after, I got a job at a very prestigious New York law firm. The rest of my life was set. Moving up the ladder to partner in my own law firm and then other firms. Moving to Larchmont, buying a starter house and then a bigger house for our three boys. Building a summer house on Cape Cod (Massachusetts still beckoned). Converting to Judaism. Welcoming five grandchildren. And living a life much more affluent and interesting than the one I left.

Not surprisingly, most of the jocks and cheerleaders stayed in Weymouth. But today they sure don't resemble the people I remember. I couldn't go to my 50th reunion, but I saw the photos. I couldn't believe that I had once achingly yearned to be part of this group.

I didn't set out to leave Weymouth, and I'm sure a lot of it has stayed with me. But I am very happy for the life that came my way after I did.

Chapter 17

LET ME DO THE COOKING

I do not do well in groups—unless I am in charge. I rankle at authority, hate hierarchies, yawn or interrupt when others drone on, and love to hear myself talk. I also am hell bent on getting things done, even if it means stepping on, or even breaking, a few toes.

When I was a boy, I had no choice about being in groups. My parents were joiners: The Democrats, the Veterans of Foreign Wars, the PTA, the Catholic Church. Find a parade and my mother was in it. Naturally, I was forced to join the junior varsity equivalents of these institutions: The Boy Scouts, the altar boys, the CYO. I wore the uniforms, learned the secret rituals and mouthed the sacred oaths; but I never got the hang of the rules or the group mentality. The priest was not happy when I stuck my hand in the golden container of the holy wafers; the nuns did not like my questioning their dogma about mortal sin which kept me up at night; and the Scoutmaster was not thrilled with my sarcastic remarks behind his back. Since I was not in charge of any of these institutions and never would be, I invested my energies in being a rebel, which was much more satisfying.

But there was a time and place when I did fit in. In the summer of '59 my parents sent me to Boy Scout Camp with my troop for a week. They also gave me a bonus: for an additional $20 I could stay for another week, without my Scoutmaster, without my troop, just me and a random bunch of other Scouts loosely supervised by boys not much older than we were. We would be living in the wild like the kids in *Lord of the Flies*, without the overwrought violence. It was perfect: no authority, no hierarchy, a leadership vacuum which I could fill and, most important, tasks that had to be done by us with little or no supervision. We pitched our tents, dug holes for latrines, gathered firewood, cooked all our meals from scratch, and created our own *a cappella* entertainment. We made rafts out of bulrushes, like the one Moses was found in as a baby. We made 24-hour baked beans, a New England staple. We dug a pit, lined it with rocks, built a roaring fire with pine and oak branches, put the raw beans, salt pork, catchup and molasses in a Dutch Oven over the coals, covered the pit and then went on a 10-mile overnight hike. Our reward: crunchy baked beans the next day for dinner, a dish that only a New Englander could love. We woke up at dawn to follow the tracks of the snakes, raccoons and foxes and add to our list of birds. And we sang and acted out "Along Came Jones," "Get a Job," and "Mother-in-Law" around the campfire at night.

Why did I like this group so much? They let me be in charge. I figured out how to build the rafts, make the beans, lip synch the songs and find the animal tracks. And I was the chef. My specialty was browned hamburger meat and onions smothered with Campbell's vegetable soup. In the woods, this was gourmet fare. (And, since I did not know any other recipes, I continued to cook this dish for years, even in Law School.) We were a group of outsiders brought together only for one week. And that made all the difference for me. Since then, I have been in many other groups but I always feel like I am the only outsider, except on the rare occasions when I have been given the reins.

Times like that fleeting week in 1959 don't happen very often, but when they do, I feel like I am on top of the world.

Chapter 18

THE VERY THIN ENVELOPE

It was a very thin envelope. I could see the light shining through it. I took it into the cemetery behind our house where I always went to be alone. There was no privacy in our tiny bandbox of a house; in the graveyard the old stone markers never asked questions. The postmark was New Haven, Connecticut. I opened the letter with trepidation.

"We are very sorry to inform you that you will not be a member of the Yale Class of 1966...." A rejection letter! But how could this be? I had crushed my SATs and was at the top of my high school class, an Ivy League guy in a blue-collar high school. But more than that, I had been bred by my parents to go to Yale; I was the vehicle for the fulfillment of their dreams.

They both grew up on the wrong side of the tracks in New Haven, geographically close but miles away in class and wealth from the Gothic towers of the Yale campus. The white shoe boys who bought their way into the College in those days poured buckets of water and rotten fruit at my father and his Irish friends as they marched through the campus on Saint Patrick's Day. Times had changed in the 30 years since then; some students were admitted on merit even without a prep school pedigree. My mother had graduated from Yale, with a Master's Degree in Education. We deluded ourselves into thinking that I was a legacy student.

I probably should have known that my chances were slim when the elderly alumnus came to call. (He could easily have been one of the boys dumping water on my father's head.) He was polite and impeccably dressed in a blue blazer and College tie, but we were from different worlds. Our conversation was awkward, and he looked around our house as if he were inspecting an Okie shack during the Depression. The interview was brief.

The day after I received the thin letter from Yale, I got a fat envelope from Brown, my "back-up school" and a place I had never even seen. I had applied on a whim, even though the $5 fee seemed extravagant since I knew I was on my way to Yale. Brown wanted me. And, although I didn't know it yet, I wanted Brown. It was in the cellar of the Ivy League; many if not most of my classmates did not come from privileged families, but from places like Brooklyn, New Jersey, Rhode Island and the down-market suburbs of Boston like mine. Public high school grads who had snuck into the Ivy League with some hard work and a lot of luck. We had a few preppies too, but they were the ones who couldn't get into Yale, Harvard or Princeton.

I grew to love Brown; it was small, challenging, and just right for me. And there was plenty of ivy to go around. I bought a Brown blazer with a 1966 on the crest, brought my flask to the football games, wrote for the Brown Daily Herald, sent monthly letters home on my Brown stationery and figured out how to succeed in class.

My parents ultimately came to realize that Brown was right for me, despite my father's futile efforts to have me embrace the Air Force ROTC. The Yale pipe dream disappeared. In its place a much better reality emerged. We are now part of the Brown family, including my brother, a cousin and my youngest son. I graduated more than 55 years ago and feel like it was just yesterday. I wish I had known in the Spring of 1962 what a blessing that thin envelope would be.

Chapter 19

ARRIVEDERCI ROMA

They get to you early. I was a couple of months old, swaddled in tight blankets, when I was committed to the Roman Catholic Church for eternity. All it took was a priest, a basin of water, and two godparents, my Dad's sister Anne and his drinking buddy Johnny, to seal the deal. No one asked me my opinion and I certainly couldn't raise my hand or speak to object.

For the next six years, I got a bit of a respite. My mother was a Methodist, so I accompanied her to Sunday School where she taught about a benign Jesus with flowing robes, long hair, a beard and a nice smile. And he was always backlighted by a glowing halo. She taught me the so-called "Old Testament" too, with its interesting stories of flooded arks, serpents, apples and the rest. I mainly played with blocks, but some of this Protestant ethos seeped in to my young brain.

But then, at seven, I reached the Catholic "age of reason." I left the benign Jesus behind and learned about mortal sin, which, unless expunged immediately, would result in eternal damnation upon my death. In those days, death always seemed imminent. My soul was figuratively a white tablet; a mortal sin, missing Mass on Sunday or telling a lie, would turn it black. A venial sin, like shoving my little brother, was less onerous. It turned my soul grey, but did not put me on the brink of damnation.

Fortunately, there was a remedy for this discoloration of my soul and the potential for eternal fire and brimstone. The Church, and only the Church, could restore that marred tablet to its original white purity. The remedy was called confession, telling the priest in a dark, secluded booth through a meshed screen, all of my sins and expressing remorse. The priest would then absolve me. The catch was that I immediately had to do penance, which usually consisted of reciting by rote 10 or 20 Hail Marys, depending on the gravity of the sins. With my soul washed clean by confession on Saturday afternoon, I could take Communion on Sunday morning, as long as I did not sin again for the next 10 hours. For a young boy, those were stressful Saturday nights!

All of these rituals were drummed into me for a whole year. My mastery of the nuances, consequences and remedies for sin made me eligible for my first communion, a very big deal for Catholics. I wore a new blue suit with a white tie, a symbol of my purity, held my hands in a prayerful tent position and kneeled in front of the priest. I was then presented with a thin dry wafer which immediately got caught in my throat. Ultimately, a piece of Jesus made it into my body and I became a new man, or boy. My family was all there, even my Methodist mom, who could not make much sense of it. They all applauded. I was on my way to Catholic nirvana.

All of this may seem ludicrous in hindsight but it was deadly serious in the 1950s. Every Wednesday we left school early to study our catechisms with the nuns. Their bodies shrouded in black robes and their faces pinched by stiff white cowls, not unlike Muslim women in abayas, they made sure that we understood the grave consequences of sin. They were particularly good at bringing the fires of hell to life. We sat in pews in the cool dark church surrounded by six-foot thick stone walls; hellfire, they said, would melt those walls and expose each of us to eternal flames. I had a very vivid imagination; getting to sleep on Wednesday nights was almost impossible. If my soul was black and I died, I would be in big trouble.

I tried to alleviate some of this anxiety by embracing the Church even more tightly. I learned Latin and became an altar boy, serving Mass every Sunday and at funerals, where I would occasionally get fifty cents, which I put in the poor box. My Irish grandmother Delia gave me a fat missal, which I read from cover to cover. Every night on my knees I would recite prayers for an hour, the Apostles Creed, more Hail Mary's and many others. These actions were my insurance policy against disaster. As was the Rosary, a ring of beads on each of which I said a prayer, repeating the cycle over and over. My grandmother was an expert at this and spent most of her free time doing it. We were very close; I was sure that when she died, she would be not be going to hell, but to its much better alternative. And, of course, like all good Catholic boys, I frequently thought of whether I had a "vocation" i.e. the right stuff to become a priest.

If there was any question about who was in charge of my life as a Catholic, it was resolved at my confirmation as a teenager. The pivotal moment in that ceremony occurs when the bishop (who I had never met before) allowed each of us to kiss his ring and then slapped us across the face. The message of where we stood in the Church was unmistakable.

The Church stayed with me even after I left home and went to College. Brown was nothing at all like my sheltered life in South Weymouth, Massachusetts. It had intellectual ferment, alcohol-fueled parties, and lots of cute girls, although the school made sex almost impossible with what they called "parietal rules"; these made the school our surrogate parents and they acted accordingly. And there were Jews, including my roommate. Until college, I had never met a Jew; South Weymouth was 75% Catholic, 25% Protestant, with not a Jew in sight. None of this had any impact on my Sunday ritual. I dutifully woke up, even with a hangover, read the Gospel at the chapel and often walked several miles to attend Mass at the Providence Cathedral. I even took a course in Catholicism.

Law school at Chicago was the same. I went to Newman Club meetings and arranged mixers with the girls from the local girls' Catholic colleges. Then I met Judy. I was in my second year of law school and she had just started her first year of social work graduate school. After two dates, she agreed to accompany me on my law firm recruiting trip to New York. We stayed at the Waldorf for six nights. I had never dated or even known a Jewish girl before. Inevitably, we began to talk about religion. It was a revelation to me. I was with a beautiful, intelligent, rational woman who did not believe in sin, hell, heaven or any of the other orthodox beliefs that I had been carrying with me for 22 years. She was a Reform Jew, who believed that when we die, what's left is the memories of us among the people we have left behind. That's it. And she was doing just fine. It took me a very long time to wrap my head around this way of thinking, but I eventually got there. I ultimately left the nuns, the priests, the beads, the missal, the sin, the hellfire and all the rest of it behind.

Thirty-five years later I became a Jew myself and said goodbye to the Church. The story of my conversion to Judaism will have to wait for another day.

Chapter 20

BOUNCED FROM THE PLANE INTO LOVE

Do we ever think about the huge role fate plays in our lives? I do, for a very special reason.

I had just turned 21 and was on my way from Boston to Chicago by plane. Although I had worked for American Airlines for two summers as a freight agent, dispatching lobsters to California and flowers to Boston—and bringing home dead soldiers from Vietnam—I had never been on a plane. In fact, I had never been west of a motel in Skaneateles NY, which was as far as my Boston-based family had traveled in our '54 Dodge. Now I was on my way to law school in Chicago and, because I had been an airline employee, I got a free plane ticket. But there was a catch. It was stand-by, which ultimately made all the difference in the world.

I felt very special leaving Boston by air wearing my tweed jacket and repp tie, looking forward to my new life in the great Midwestern metropolis. I even treated myself to a cocktail. But Chicago was not our first stop; on this flight we had to touch down in Rochester to pick up more Chicago-bound passengers. Unfortunately, all of them had paid for their tickets, which meant that the only standby (me) had to get off and wait for the next plane. I had plenty of time, so the delay didn't bother me. Unlike today, spending five hours in a small, unfamiliar airport was an adventure, not an irritant.

While I waited, I saw another guy in a tweed jacket and tie who looked like he was on his way to my destination. I introduced myself. His name was David and he was in fact heading to business school at the same university. He had gone to school in Rochester and was recovering from a tearful goodbye to Alice, his college girlfriend. She was a senior and would be spending another year in Rochester before joining David in Chicago. David was smitten with Alice and spent all of our time at the airport, on the plane, at our hotel and on the way to school telling me about how much he loved her, how beautiful and smart she was, and how they were going to spend the rest of their lives together. I was very affected by everything David said. I had just broken up with my college girlfriend, so I was envious of David and Alice and hoped one day to be able to experience the same passion.

I saw David from time to time over the school year and in the following summer in New York. To my surprise, he told me just before we went back to school that his romance with Alice had faded, which was awkward since she was on her way to Chicago to be with him after her graduation. They were still friends but David had apparently moved on. I could not resist. I had to meet Alice. I got her phone number from David and she agreed to go with me to the law school mixer. She also asked me to get dates for the dance for her classmate and the classmate's friend, who was going to social work graduate school. I said "of course" and found two very willing guys to join us.

My relationship with Alice did not last more than one night; but the social work student, Oh my! Judy and I came from two different worlds. She was from New York, I was from New England; she was Jewish, I was Catholic; she wore tailored clothes from Best & Co, I wore a torn rugby shirt; she was sophisticated, I was very rough around the edges. Like Billy Joel's song, she was an "uptown girl" and I was a downtown guy. But who can explain love or fate? I pursued her and she was (thank goodness) willing to be pursued.

After 54 years, three children and five grandchildren, we are still together. None of this would have happened if I had not been bumped from that plane in Rochester. Although I don't fly stand-by any more, I am always ready to be bumped again in life. You never know where it will lead.

Chapter 21

THANK YOU JACKIE O!

Our parents knew we were getting married even before we did. Judy and I had met at a Law School mixer in October, 1967. The attraction was instantaneous. She liked the torn rugby shirt under my Harris Tweed jacket and I liked everything about her, her style, elegance, dignity and good looks. She survived dinner at the card table in our ramshackle bachelor apartment; by contrast, when I came to pick her up, she served cheese and crackers in her stylish, modern apartment.

When Christmas vacation arrived, the only facts our parents had were that Judy was dating a Catholic guy, a first for her, and I was dating a Jew, a first for me. We were both goody-goodies, first born children who were frighteningly compliant with our parents' wishes, and high achievers. There must have been something in the tone of our voices during phone calls or the situation itself that set off alarm bells in Westfield, NJ and South Weymouth, MA. We were in a battle to save our relationship even before we knew how far it was going.

We visited each other's homes for the holidays. I went first. I hitched a ride to New York and we had dinner with Judy's college roommate and her boyfriend at V&T, a venerable Italian dive near Columbia with cheap wine and lots of red sauce. We then took a bus from the Port Authority Terminal to Westfield, where we were met by Judy's younger sister Alice. Judy's parents were asleep but I did meet her father soon enough. Anxiety, wine and too much red sauce got to me in the middle of the night. I met Leon as I was heaving my guts into the toilet bowl. Leon brought me a glass of brandy; no editorializing, just practical help. But I could not help but think of the drunken Irish Catholic stereotype I was confirming in his mind. Addie was sweet; she made sure the fridge was stocked with plenty of ham, mayo and white bread. Sadie, Addie's mother, who came out from Borough Park, Brooklyn, every weekend, was less sweet. She called me a "sheigetz" (a non-Jewish boy) and muttered other less than endearing Yiddish terms for me under her breath. Making out in the living room was a challenge. The dominant figure in the room was a large statue of Moses, holding the tablets, and looking straight at me with a baleful stare.

Judy's trip to South Weymouth for Christmas was just as unsettling for her. The house was filled with Christmas paraphernalia which my Mom excitedly put out every year: the tree, the crèche, the candles in the windows, the wreath, the presents. But this was not really a joyful Christmas for Mom because she anticipated that, if I married this girl, Christmas, Easter, and all the rest of her family's intact Christian culture would be coming to an end. Maybe that's why, when Judy and I arrived in the afternoon from Logan Airport, Mom was asleep on the couch. Judy never forgot this greeting. My father, on the other hand, was superficially charming. He liked pretty young girls and was happy to entertain Judy, but as soon as she left the room, the hammer came down on me. Judy dutifully went to Mass, exchanged presents, and went through all the motions. We were both very happy to get back to school.

After Christmas, our respective parents began a six-month campaign to talk each of us out of marrying outside of our faiths. There were tears, threats, visits to priests and rabbis, references to the Holocaust and the Irish potato famine, and constant assaults on what to us was the most natural thing in the world. None of it worked.

The following summer we lived together in a fourth-floor walkup on West 75th Street, just off Central Park. For parental consumption, Judy was living there with a friend and I was sharing an apartment with my college roommate. One morning at 7 am, I answered the phone; it was Judy's mother, asking for her. Neither Judy nor I said a word; all Judy's mother heard was my stifled breaths. I guess our parents knew more than they were letting on. Their lobbying went on all summer; the marriage was a certainty, but each side wanted to do it their own way. Judy's sanctimonious rabbi would not marry us unless I converted, a pre-condition I rejected. My parents hauled me off to their Monsignor friend in Connecticut. His message was the same. There would be no wedding unless we were both Catholic. This pronouncement was accompanied by a not so subtle message about the dire consequences that would befall me if I married outside of the faith. This news was ironic, since it was delivered by a man who was clearly gay.

Judy and I argued incessantly about all of this; one or both of us stormed out of restaurants, slammed the apartment door, stomped through Central Park for hours, cried incessantly, and in my case, obfuscated. Judy and I had agreed that on my next visit I would tell my parents that I would not go along with their plans, but I just couldn't. She was livid. However, despite all the heartache and drama, we always came back together. The battles with our parents, which neither of us had ever engaged in before, made us a stronger couple and slowly, incrementally, forged an unbreakable bond.

The denouement was our last visit to my parents just before we went back to Chicago. We had all our worldly goods in an open U-Haul trailer and were ready to move in to married student housing and get married in November. For my parents, this was their last stand. The visit was like a Shiva call. They acted as if the son they knew had died and they were in mourning. It was horrible. When we were finally on our way, outside of Buffalo, the heavens opened and drenched everything we owned. The tears had followed us all the way from South Weymouth. But we were a couple now. There was no turning back. We dried everything out and bought a tarp for the rest of trip. We were beginning to learn together how to cope with the indignities that life threw our way.

We found a very nice Unitarian minister to marry us in Chicago. No parents were there. But Judy's parents planned a reception for us in New Jersey and invited John and Virginia to attend. Although the four of them did not want to witness the marriage, three of them seemed willing to celebrate a *fait accompli*. Except my father, who initially refused to come.

Here is where Jackie O comes in. In the fall of 1968, Jackie had decided to marry Aristotle Onassis, who was definitely not a Roman Catholic. Catholics in Boston were buzzing about this sacrilege. But Cardinal Cushing, who was a family hero, said it was okay for Jackie to marry Ari. This gave my father the cover he needed to change his mind. In his warped view, if Jackie could marry a Greek Orthodox guy, it was okay for him to attend a reception honoring his son's marriage to a Jew.

Judy, her sister, my brother, my college roommate, and I all flew from Chicago to New Jersey. Leon rolled out a red carpet at 7 Plymouth Road. Addie threw a great party. Friends and family gathered around as we cut the huge cake. Judy was a beautiful bride, even without the long white dress. And I could barely remember a thing that happened, other than the fake smile plastered on my face the whole time.

Postscript

78 YEARS OF FOUR-LEAF CLOVERS

When I was a young lad, my Irish Catholic grandmother Delia convinced me that there was a pot of gold at the end of every rainbow, guarded by a leprechaun. My brothers and I spent hours on our bikes chasing rainbows looking for that leprechaun and his gold. Delia also told us about the magical powers of four-leaf clovers. They brought the finder immense amounts of good luck. We scoured the grassy patch in front of our house for hours searching for these rare tiny plants. Every once in a while, one would turn up and I'd be ecstatic.

My 78th birthday will soon be here. As I reflect on my life over three quarters of a century, I believe it has been protected by acres of Delia's bright green four-leaf clovers, real or figurative. My good fortune is boundless.

I was born on July 31, 1945 near an Army base in Terre Haute Indiana. My father had returned from the war in Europe the prior summer and always said he was being "fattened up" for the planned land invasion of Japan. A few weeks after I was born, Japan surrendered. Dad did not have to go back to war and I did not have to risk losing my father.

I was lucky in my choice of parents. Mom was a highly moral Yankee school teacher who ran a tight ship filled with three unruly sons and a husband who liked to drink too much, probably to forget what his life had been like on the front lines in North Africa, Sicily and Italy. We had no car or TV but we had a large collection of leather-bound classic books: *Les Miserables, The Three Musketeers, Oliver Twist,* all of Shakespeare's plays and sonnets, *The Rubaiyat of Omar Khayyam,* and many more. Mom meticulously placed a label, "Ex Libris The Delehantys," in each one. These books, and the words they contained, were a large part of my childhood universe.

School was a breeze. I brought home a large harvest of "A's" every few months written in blue ink on stiff cardboard cards. Anything less than an A was unacceptable. In second grade I wrote my autobiography. The principal told me to go straight to fourth grade; there was nothing new I could learn in third. Here the clovers may have faltered a little bit. I spent the rest of my school days relying on intuition rather than sweat. My precocity could only take me so far.

However, intuition did have a substantial upside. I was very good at multiple choice tests, where the choice among A, B, C, D and E always seemed pretty obvious. Although my grades were so-so, my test scores were excellent. The clovers abounded. I went to Brown, a college that was way above my head, and, even more amazing, the University of Chicago Law School, one of the best in the country. And Chicago was free. I got a special scholarship and did not pay a dime for three years.

Chicago was a field of clover. I met Judy there. The chemistry was instantaneous even though we came from different worlds. The only explanation for her attraction to me was that little green plant. I wore a torn rugby shirt, from a game I didn't play; she wore Bonwit Teller. I was Oscar; she was Felix. She was a Jew; I was a Catholic. We fought a war with our parents to get married. We won. She has sustained me for more than 55 years, enabling me to feel like a patriarch, with three sons, four grandsons and Daisy, a rare Delehanty girl. Our boys are loving fathers. I am thankful to have broken the chain of bad fathering with which I grew up.

Chicago also gave me a career. I charmed my way into a position at Paul Weiss, one of the best firms in New York. Paul Weiss paved the way for my starting my own firm, and for partnerships at other equally prestigious firms in the City. I now mediate and can draw upon 50 years of litigation experience to help weary litigants settle their differences. I am making up for all the trouble I caused as a lawyer.

Much of the above is overshadowed by the greatest stroke of luck in my life. I have a congenital kidney disease, which I inherited from my Mom. Generations of her McDonald family have succumbed at early ages to kidney failure and strokes, my grandfather at age 45. When I was in my mid-50s, I needed a new kidney. Judy had an incompatible blood type and my two brothers had an early form of the same disease. I needed a miracle. And I got one. Jim Smith, the husband of one of Judy's college classmates, called out of the blue and offered me one of his. Twenty-one years later it is still going strong.

Being almost 78 is not for the meek. The litany of maladies can make me feel like Job, when I can't resist wallowing in self-pity: polycystic kidney disease, squamous cell carcinoma, branch vein retinal occlusion, Dupuytren's contracture, enlarged prostate—to name just a few.

None of it matters. The good fortune that has buttressed me all these years is not going away. Delia is still fingering her rosary beads in heaven and four-leaf clovers still appear. I am ready for whatever lies ahead.

Acknowledgements

This book grew out of a series of memoir classes I attended at the Hudson Valley Writers Center in Sleepy Hollow, NY. I want to thank my teachers there, Susan Hodara and Mindy Lewis, for their astute critiques of my writing, as well as the many students who gave me valuable feedback during class. I also want to thank Mindy for editing this book.

I also want to thank my illustrator, Justine Yeung, whose inspired art brought these chapters to life.

My thanks also to my wife Judy and and my brothers Hugh and Dennis who inspired many of these stories and to my three sons with whom I shared many of these memories.

New Rochelle, NY
May 25, 2023